Goldfish

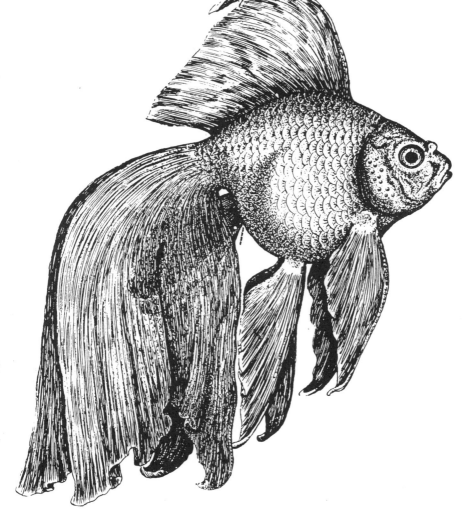

by Joseph Roberts

This book was originally published as Goldfish for Beginners; *this present edition has been enlarged and enhanced with completely new illustrations and magnificent color photographs.*

Distributed in the UNITED STATES by T.F.H. Publications, Inc., One T.F.H. Plaza, Neptune City, NJ 07753; in CANADA to the Pet Trade by H & L Pet Supplies Inc., 27 Kingston Crescent, Kitchener, Ontario N2B 2T6; Rolf C. Hagen Ltd., 3225 Sartelon Street, Montreal 382 Quebec; in CANADA to the Book Trade by Macmillan of Canada (A Division of Canada Publishing Corporation), 164 Commander Boulevard, Agincourt, Ontario M1S 3C7; in ENGLAND by T.F.H. Publications Limited, Cliveden House/Priors Way/Bray, Maidenhead, Berkshire SL6 2HP, England; in AUSTRALIA AND THE SOUTH PACIFIC by T.F.H. (Australia) Pty. Ltd., Box 149, Brookvale 2100 N.S.W., Australia; in NEW ZEALAND by Ross Haines & Son, Ltd., 18 Monmouth Street, Grey Lynn, Auckland 2, New Zealand; in the PHILIPPINES by Bio-Research, 5 Lippay Street, San Lorenzo Village, Makati Rizal; in SOUTH AFRICA by Multipet Pty. Ltd., 30 Turners Avenue, Durban 4001. Published by T.F.H. Publications, Inc. Manufactured in the United States of America by T.F.H. Publications, Inc.

Contents

Color photography—Dr. Herbert R. Axelrod, Michael Gilroy, courtesy of Midori Shobo, and Fred Rosenzweig.

Japanese Veiltail, top view.

Introduction

Goldfish today are such a common sight on the American scene that it is difficult to realize that just a bit over a century ago they were virtually unknown to this country, the first being brought to these shores from Japan by Admiral Ammon in 1874. Originally cultivated in the Orient by Korean, Chinese, and Japanese breeders, the specimens brought to this country were almost immediately popular, and by 1890 commercial fisheries were in operation in the United States.

These Oriental breeders developed the present-day ornamental pet from a member of the carp family, *Carassius auratus*. Some of today's goldfish

A Pearlscale Telescope Goldfish.

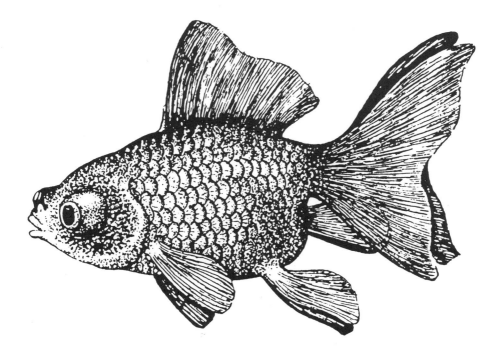

5

may be able to trace their family tree to the European goldfish, *Carassius carassius,* which is thought to have been crossed with cultivated types of the Asiatic stock. However, none of the ornamental goldfish were developed solely from this European representative of the carp family.

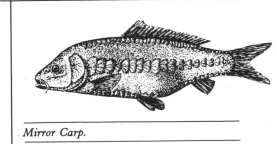

Mirror Carp.

In their natural state, both kinds of goldfish are a silver-gray or olive hue in color, but they have a strong tendency toward xanthism, which produces occasional specimens of a yellow or golden color. The Oriental breeders through selective breeding fixed these colors so that only occasionally do you find a mature goldfish which retains the original goldfish coloring.

While there are quite a few different colors and shapes of goldfish, all goldfish can be classified as either scaled or matte ("scaleless"). Scaled goldfish can be identified by the metallic luster of their colors, which are usually red, white, olive-gray, or black. Most of the goldfish you find in stores today are scaled. All of the scaled goldfish pass through a period when they are smoke-colored and are called silverfish, but they later change to one of the colors cited above.

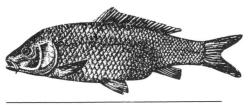

Scaled Carp raised in quantity in Europe for food.

"Scaleless" goldfish actually do have scales, but these are so transparent that they are barely perceptible. These matte fish lack the metallic luster of the scaled goldfish, but they are found in a greater variety of colors, including two not found in the scaled variety—blue and

Goldfish In The Aquarium

lavender tints—and the colors are more refined. The scaleless fish differ from the scaled also in that they do not go through the period of being silverfish but commence to develop their permanent colors at about six weeks. The first color is white sprinkled with black specks. One objection to the transparently-scaled fish is that the rays of the fins are weak, the dorsal fin and tail drooping soon after they become fully developed.

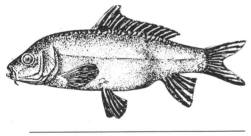

A carp without scales is called a Leather Carp. Goldfish and carp are very closely related.

Given proper care, something that millions of common goldfish fail to receive, they should live from ten to twenty years in an aquarium. In ponds, goldfish have lived more than thirty years, so you can see that Nature has endowed the goldfish with a capacity for long life so long as man does not deprive it of a normal opportunity to realize that expectancy.

The Aquarium Versus the Bowl

Your first problem to be solved after you decide to keep goldfish is the selection of a proper container for your fish.

Since one of the most common causes of goldfish losses is probably overcrowding, you must first decide how many fish you would like to keep. A good rule of thumb for determining how many fish can be kept safely in an aquarium is to allow twenty square inches of surface for each one-inch fish, sixty square inches for each two-inch fish, 120 square inches for each three-inch fish, and 240 square inches of surface area for each four-inch fish. In measuring your fish do not include the tail fin. You may determine the surface area of the aquarium by multiplying the length times the width.

Goldfish In The Aquarium

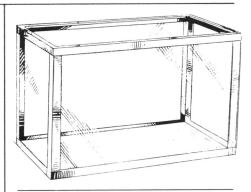

A fish bowl for goldfish is obsolete and impractical. They crack, distort the view of the fish and are extremely difficult to clean.

Frameless aquariums have all but replaced the framed aquariums, though plastic-framed aquariums are making a comeback.

Goldfish In The Aquarium

In the minds of most beginners there is no distinction between a bowl and an aquarium, but the bowl is scorned by most aquarists and described as the poorest type of container for a fish. They object to a bowl because: (1) it does not have a large enough contact area between air and water, and therefore the water cannot absorb enough oxygen from the air to supply the fish's needs; (2) the rounded sides magnify the fish and make them appear distorted when seen through the glass; (3) the rounded sides reflect the light toward the center in a manner that annoys the fish; (4) the rounded bottom prevents natural decorating; (5) such a bowl cannot be repaired if broken; (6)

Modern all-glass aquariums are available in many shapes and sizes with fitting and matching covers and lights.

Goldfish In The Aquarium

Your local petshop will have magnificent aquariums of all sizes and dimensions to fit into almost any decor.

Goldfish In The Aquarium

it is not large enough to support growing plants; (7) the water must be changed frequently, which is bad for the fish; (8) the water temperature fluctuates rapidly; (9) the water easily becomes polluted; and (10) the bowl cannot be easily balanced.

Fish fanciers give the following reasons for favoring the aquarium: (1) large contact area between air and water; (2) straight sides give a clear view of the fish; (3) flat bottom on which natural conditions can be arranged; (4) an aquarium lends itself well to the use of growing plants; (5) water temperature does not fluctuate rapidly; (6) the

Goldfish do very well in square or rectangular tanks, too. The models shown here were originally designed as terrariums, but the air holes in the cover help circulate air in the water if no pump or filter is used.

aquarium may be repaired when broken; (7) the larger size ensures more fish in better health; (8) better display of fish, plants, and scavengers; (9) fish can be bred and raised under observation.

No other accommodation for living things is as easily adjusted to the confines of a small apartment nor as easy to maintain as an aquarium stocked with fish and plants.

Goldfish In The Aquarium

Buying the Necessary Supplies

The first item on your list of supplies is, of course, the aquarium. Buy the largest you can afford. Remember that the

The aquariums come fitted with stands and covers. The covers may have a light built into them.

Goldfish In The Aquarium

larger the tank the better your chances for healthy fish. A large tank will keep a more even water temperature than a small one and thus increase the likelihood of successfully breeding fish.

Although plants will provide some oxygen for your fish and scavengers will eat some of the debris, you should play safe by purchasing an air pump and a filter for your aquarium. Your pet shop will have many types of each on display at prices ranging from under $5 to $50 or more. It is probably best to buy a good, medium-priced model of each that will fit your aquarium and allow you to increase the number of fish at a later date. Your pet shop dealer can advise you on what is best for your goals and budget.

After the aquarium and equipment have been purchased, the next step will be to obtain the sand to cover its bottom. Washed fine sand or gravel of exactly the right size can be bought at any pet shop. Buy enough sand to cover the bottom of your tank two inches thick at the back sloping down to an inch at the front.

Avoid using marbles or large particles of gravel as decorations in the aquarium. Bits of food may become lodged between the marbles or gravel beyond the reach of the fish and decay, causing the water to grow foul.

The selection and purchase of plants for your tank are very important. Plants serve a threefold purpose: they furnish beauty, oxygen, and a breeding place for fish. With these purposes in mind select your plants with care. You will probably find the pet shop dealer very helpful in choosing your supplies.

Remember that when your aquarium is outfitted with a pump and a filter you will not need live plants to provide oxygen for the fish. Plants do make the aquarium look nice, but they are not really essential. Plastic plants that are very life-like are available.

Vallisneria is a good oxygenator and is very hardy and prolific; its grass-like appearance makes a very nice background, but it is not recommended for a small

Goldfish In The Aquarium

You can start with an aquarium and stand and later add a separate cover with built-in light and an air pump.

Goldfish In The Aquarium

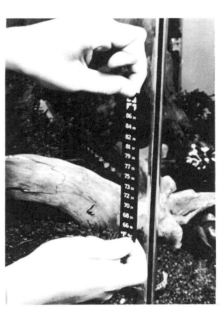

Additional accessories for your goldfish tank are strip thermometers, platforms which attach to the aquarium to hold various accessories, and various water test kits.

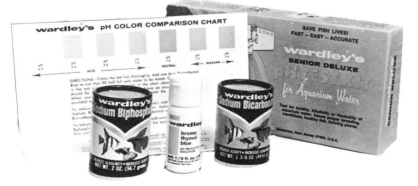

Goldfish In The Aquarium

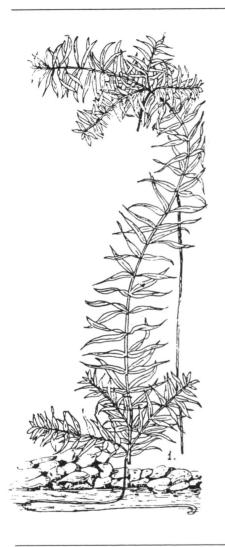

aquarium.

Sagittaria, another grass-like plant, is highly recommended as a good oxygenator and a hardy grower. It also can be used as a background.

There are several varieties of plants that do well when planted in clusters, adding a distinctive touch to the aquarium. These plants are usually bought in bunches. They include *Elodea, Myriophyllum, Ludwigia,* parrot feather, and *Cabomba.*

The most common goldfish bunch plant is called Elodea *or* Ditchweed. *It grows thinner or more dense depending upon the light it receives.*

Opposite: *A group of peacock tail goldfish, also known as "jikin." Members of this race should have a white body with red lips and fins. However, specimens with proper markings are rare.*

A pair of six-month-old calico veiltail goldfish. Veiltails originated in the US and are characterized by their long anal fins, squared-off caudal fins, and the high dorsal fin.

The lionhead goldfish is also known as the buffalohead. Lionheads are noted for the raspberry-like growth that covers the head and gill plates.

A young oranda goldfish. Some breeders believe the oranda originated from a cross between a lionhead and a fantail, but this point is still being debated.

A strawberry oranda goldfish. Note the striking contrast between the body color and that of the head growth.

A fantail goldfish. Fantails have long been among the most popular goldfish varieties.

A pair of champion lionhead gold-fish. One way to tell the relative age of a lionhead is to look at the size of its growth.

A group of common American goldfish. The coloration of the younger, smaller fish will change as they age.

Goldfish In The Aquarium

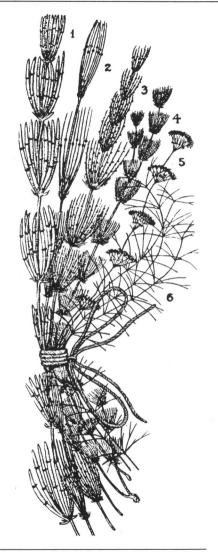

Six representative stone algae are: 1. Chara coronate; *2.* Nitella Flexilis; *3.* Chara gymnopus; *4.* Chara crinita; *5.* Nitella tenuissima; *6.* Nitella gracilis.

If your aquarium is large enough you will want to select some outstanding plant to feature in the center of your underwater landscape. Spatterdock, cryptocorynes, or an underwater fern such as the water sprite may be used. These larger plants should be planted in small pots, using a little soil covered with gravel. Unless your aquarium is large, however, I would not recommend using any potted plants.

A very attractive addition to your aquarium is hair grass; when properly started it will form a regular carpet on the bottom of the tank. After you have the aquarium stocked, you may want to include some floating plants such as the shell flower, water lettuce, or the water fern.

Don't be confused by the different plants listed. Your first purchase should be limited to only those plants that are to be planted in the sand on the bottom, the others to come later.

The next item on your list of supplies for the balanced aquarium is the cleanup squad.

Goldfish In The Aquarium

Eel grass, Vallisneria spiralis, *often called Corkscrew Val, is an ideal plant for the goldfish tank which gets a lot of light.*

Sagittaria natans, *or Broad-Leafed Sag.*

Goldfish In The Aquarium

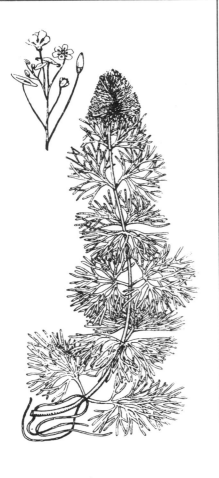

Scavengers are the buzzards of the aquarium world; they go about the tank eating waste food and excess vegetable matter and thus help to keep the aquarium clean.

The most popular scavengers are the snails, but not all kinds of snails. Some are so large that they use up more oxygen than the fish.

Our native pond snail is as desirable a scavenger as can be found. It is a good workman, picking up surplus food and cleaning the side glass of algae. It does not attack the plants so long as it can find other food. Under suitable conditions it will deposit its egg cases either on the glass or on the water plants, and its young will readily hatch.

Cabomba caroliniana, *above; below: three kinds of duckweed. 1.* Lemna minor; *2.* Lemna trisulca; *3.* Spirodella polyrhiza.

Two views of the Georgia snail, Viviparus georgianus.

Four views of Lymnaea stagnalis.

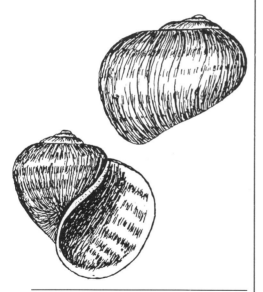

The Apple Snail, Ampullaria depressa, two views.

The most common aquarium snail is Planorbis, shown here in four views.

Goldfish In The Aquarium

Red and black ramshorn snails are very attractive eaters of algae and will do very well in your tank. They are also prolific and will breed under suitable conditions. The Japanese trapdoor snail is very decorative.

When buying scavengers you must, as always, keep in mind the size of your tank. Too many scavengers lose their value as the cleanup squad and become a liability rather than an asset. Dead snails decay and cause the water to become polluted. The best method is to buy only a few scavengers at first and add to your collection as they are needed.

With the purchase of a few fish, you will have all the necessary equipment to set up an aquarium. There are, however, other items that should be added to your list which will help you in caring for your fish.

A small dip net is very handy in handling your stock. Be sure that the net is good and deep.

A glass feeding ring will help to keep the tank clean by confining the food in one spot.

A siphon tube is very useful in

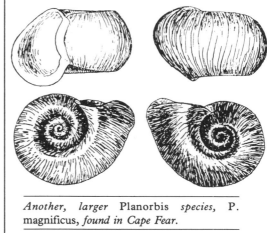

Another, larger Planorbis *species,* P. magnificus, *found in Cape Fear.*

The Japanese snail, Viviparus malleatus.

The Transparent African Snail, Lymnaea auricularia.

Goldfish In The Aquarium

changing the water. Several yards of small plastic tubing will serve very well, or you may be able to purchase one of the self-starting siphons that eliminate the necessity of filling the tube by drawing on it with your lips.

A dip tube is handy in removing excess food or dead snails from the bottom of the tank.

If your aquarium does not have a glass cover you should buy one. A glass cover keeps dust and soot from falling on the water surface and keeps lively fish from jumping out. It also helps to hold the water temperature at an even level.

You also will need one or two accurate thermometers to aid you in keeping a check on the water temperature.

Setting up an Aquarium

Your first step in setting up your aquarium is to wash your tank thoroughly with clear water to which a little salt has been added. Don't use soap or any kind of cleaning powder. The

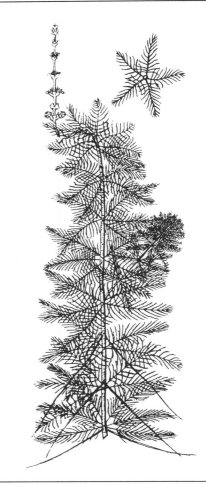

Myriophyllum spicatum *is the Spiked Water Milfoil. It is a wonderful plant for the goldfish tank that gets a lot of light.*

Goldfish In The Aquarium

Marsh Purslane, Ludwigia palustris, *is a very common goldfish aquarium plant, but unless it gets a great deal of light it falls apart.*

slight abrasive action of the salt will remove any grease or dirt that may have gathered on the tank during handling. After a thorough washing and rinsing, polish the tank dry with a soft clean rag.

Your next step is to select a suitable location. This is especially important if you have decided on living plants, as light is essential for the health of your plants. Plants cannot grow and give off oxygen unless they have several hours of strong indirect light each day. If you use artificial plants the aquarium can be put in almost any non-drafty spot that will safely support its weight and not be in the way.

The best location for a well-planted tank is near a window facing east, where the aquarium will receive the morning sunlight. If you cannot use an eastern window, the next best is a southern or western exposure.

Let your aquarium have all the strong indirect light possible, but very little direct light. If the sun is too strong and overheats the water, shield the aquarium by putting special backing paper on the outside of the back glass.

Goldfish In The Aquarium

Your aquarium will probably appear to its best advantage if you use artificial light. Lighted hoods that use either incandescent or fluorescent light are made to fit all aquaria and often come attached to the glass aquarium cover you bought earlier. If the plants thrive you may be sure the light is sufficient. Too much light increases the algal growth and makes the water look green. Insufficient light causes the water to look brown.

The next requirement for the location of your aquarium is that the stand on which it will rest must be level and support the bottom at all points. No upward pressure should be put directly against the bottom as this tends to separate the bottom from the sides. The foundation should be steady and permanent.

Mount your aquarium on a secure stand. Someone might accidentally tip it over or it might break if the foundation is not secure.

Goldfish In The Aquarium

Mermaid Weed, Proserpinaca palustris, *a nice plant for the goldfish aquarium.*

After you have selected your location, support the aquarium with both hands beneath the bottom and carry it to the spot selected. Do not carry an aquarium from the top or it will eventually spring the sides away from each other and cause leaks.

Place the tank firmly on the stand and test it to see that it is level and that the foundation on which the tank rests is solid and able to support the added weight of a filled tank. Always fill your aquarium at its permanent location. Never move it after it is filled or it may develop leaks.

The air pump and filter should now be set up, especially if you are using a filter that goes on the bottom of the tank under the sand or gravel. Make sure all the power cords will safely reach an outlet and that you have enough plastic tubing to run the equipment.

Next cover the bottom of your tank with sand or gravel. Never put sand, plants, or ornaments into your tank without first washing them. The best way to wash sand is to place it in a clean bucket or pan and run hot or cold water over it until it is clean. You may have to wash the sand several times to free it of dust. Be sure the sand is perfectly clean or your aquarium will be cloudy.

Cover the bottom of the tank with the sand, sloping it from

Goldfish In The Aquarium

the back and sides toward the front center, allowing two inches at the back and sides and an inch at the front. The movement of the water will cause the excess dirt and waste matter to accumulate at the lowest point in the front where it can be easily removed with a dip tube or siphon.

After arranging the sand you are ready to put in your first plants if you are using them. First sterilize the plants by washing them in a strong solution of salt water to remove any parasites that might be harmful to the fish.

Put about two inches of water in the tank to hold the sand in place while you set the plants. Proper arrangement will add to the beauty of your aquarium and show the fish off to better advantage.

Keep the plants in a pan of fresh water until you are ready to put them in the tank so that they won't dry out. Scoop out a hole in the sand and set your plants as deeply as possible, but be sure to leave the crown (the point from which the leaves start growing)

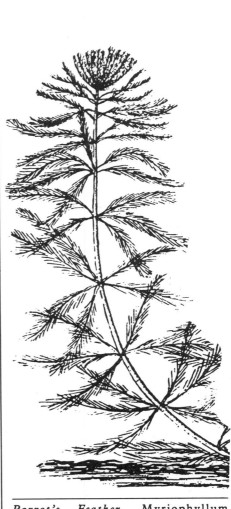

Parrot's Feather, Myriophyllum proserpinacoides.

Goldfish In The Aquarium

slightly exposed. Plants breathe from the crown, and if buried too deeply they will suffocate.

Cover the roots as well as you can. You will find that a pencil is very handy to help push the roots deep into the sand. Arrange your landscape with the tallest plants in the back and smaller ones in front. Set the plants along the back and sides as thickly as you like but leave the front of the tank unobstructed to

The Madagascar Laceplant is very, very difficult to raise unless it gets a great of light. The same is true of the Giant Anacharis shown below. Anacharis is very inexpensive, while the Lace Plant is probably the most expensive of water plants for the aquarium.

allow free swimming room for the fish. There isn't any danger of having too many plants as long as there is enough light and ample room for the fish to swim.

After all the plants are in place, siphon off the water and refill the tank with fresh water. If some of the plants float loose, push them back into place with a pencil.

Goldfish In The Aquarium

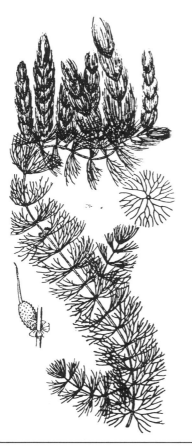

Hornwort, Ceratophyllum demersum, *is a beautiful plant for the goldfish aquarium.*

Mulertt's Ludwigia is very difficult to keep in an aquarium unless it gets direct sunlight for a few hours every day.

Regular city water from the faucet can be used, provided it has been aged for twelve hours or more and treated with an anti-chlorine chemical.

Fill the tank to within two inches of the top and let it stand for several hours before putting in the scavengers. The easiest way to fill your tank without stirring up the sand is to place a baffle of some sort on the bottom. A clean piece of heavy

Goldfish In The Aquarium

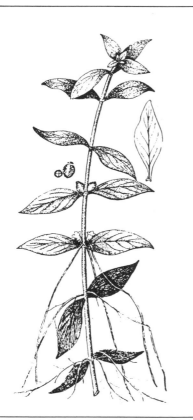

Cylindric-fruited Ludwigia, Ludwigia glandulosa.

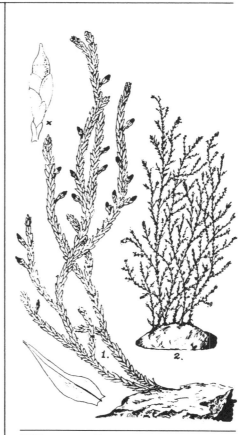

Willowmoss. Two species are kept: 1. Fontinalis antipyretica *and 2.* Fontinalis gracilis.

wrapping paper or cardboard may be used to pour the water on. Pour the water slowly and remove the paper as soon as the tank is filled.

It is best to let the water season for about a week before introducing the fish. This gives time for the plants to take root and gives you time to check your equipment to see that everything is in working order. If you use an air pump and filter, the aquarium may have to stand only a day or two before adding fish, especially if you use plastic plants.

Goldfish thrive in temperatures between 65 and 70 degrees F, but they can survive a wide range of temperatures—as high as 90 degrees and as low as 34 degrees. For this reason, heaters and thermostats are usually unnecessary for the aquarium which is to be devoted solely to goldfish, although they are handy as insurance during the winter and to help make sure the temperature stays stable.

Floating Pondweed, Potamogeton densus, *is sometimes available for the aquarium.*

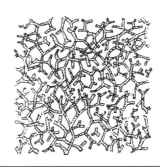

Riccia fluitans, *Crystalwort, is a nice top covering. Some goldfish eat it.*

How to Choose Goldfish

The knack of buying only healthy fish of the right size and desirable color is simple to learn and may save you from later regrets and difficulties. Stand in front of the dealer's display tank and watch the fish for a few minutes. Note which fish are the most active and have the brightest colors. Active fish of bright color and with an erect dorsal fin (this is the fin on top of the body) are usually healthy.

Don't buy fish that swim on their sides, swim sluggishly near the top of the water, lie on the bottom of the aquarium, or scrape their sides along its bottom.

The Right Goldfish For You

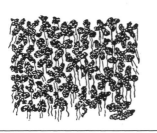

Floating Pondmoss, Azolla caroliniana, is a suitable floating plant. It cuts down on top sunlight.

Having tentatively chosen a fish, examine it carefully. If the fish is coated with heavy scum or tiny white dots, beware—it is probably sick and should not be purchased.

By purchasing your fish stock and supplies from a reliable dealer you will eliminate much of the risk.

Varieties of Goldfish

When you reach the point where you must decide which variety or varieties of goldfish you will keep, you will be surprised at the many fascinating kinds of goldfish available. Most stores that sell fish offer five or six kinds to choose from—

Spring Waterstarwort, Callitriche verna.

The Right Goldfish For You

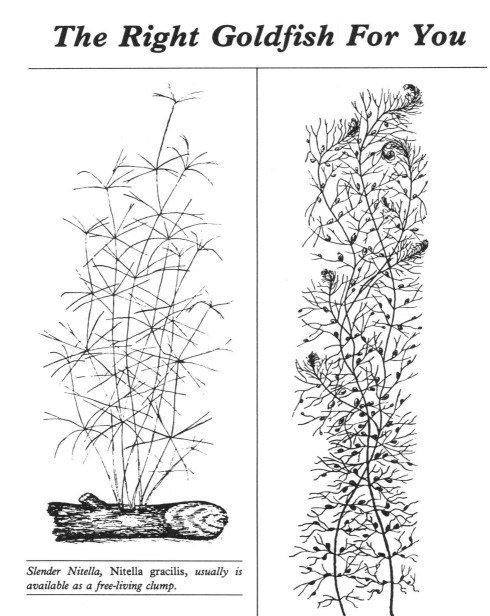

Slender Nitella, Nitella gracilis, *usually is available as a free-living clump.*

Bladderwort, Utricularia biflora, *should not be used for spawning, as the fry may get trapped in the bladders.*

The Right Goldfish For You

Greater Bladderwort, above, and Lesser Bladderwort, lower plant.

Mare's Tail, Hippuris vulgaris, *is a strong and hardy plant if it receives enough daily sunlight. This is uncommonly found in aquarium shops now since more beautiful plants are available for the goldfish tank.*

The Right Goldfish For You

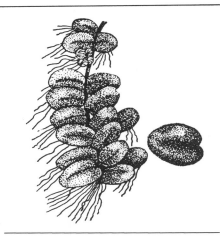

Two floating plants. Salvinia *above, and* Trianea *below.*

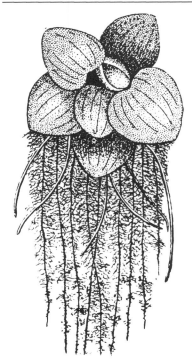

Curled-leaved Pondweed, shown above, while the lower plant is Spear-leaved Pondweed, both of the genus Potamogeton.

The Right Goldfish For You

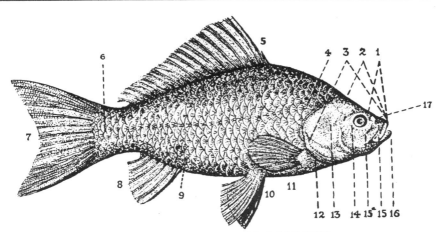

COMMON AMERICAN GOLDFISH

Common American Goldfish

1) Snout. 2) Distance from snout to nape, or occiput. 3) Head. 4) Lateral line. 5) Dorsal fin. 6) Base of caudal fin. 1 to 6) Distance from snout to base of caudal fin. 7) Caudal fin. 8) Anal fin.

9) Anus. 10) Ventral fin. 11) Pectoral fin. 12) Branchiostegals. 13) Operculum. 14) Eye. 15) Upper jaw, or maxillary. 15a) Preorbital. 16) Lower jaw, or mandible. 17) Nostril.

---

comets, shubunkins, moors, telescopes, and fantails. You'll probably want some of each, but don't waste money on more fish than you can provide with ample room in which to live. Too many fish or too large fish will crowd a small tank, with the result that you will lose most or all of them. Brief descriptions of the more popular varieties follow.

COMMON GOLDFISH: This variety is closely related to the original stock (*Carassius auratus*) and has most of its characteristics. It is quite similar to the cultivated carp or koi (*Cyprinus carpio*) but lacks the barbel which the koi has at each corner of its mouth. A very hardy fish capable of enduring wide extremes of temperature

43

The Right Goldfish For You

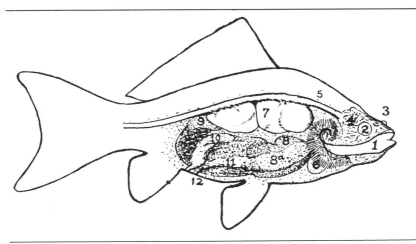

Interior anatomy of the Goldfish, showing parts referred to in descriptions.
1) Gullet and gills. 2) Eye socket. 3) Nasal passage. 4) Brain. 5) Vertebrae. 6) Heart. 7) Swim-bladder. 8) Liver. 8a)Stomach. 9) Kidney. 10) Testis. 11) Intestines. 12) Anus.

The skeleton of the common goldfish.

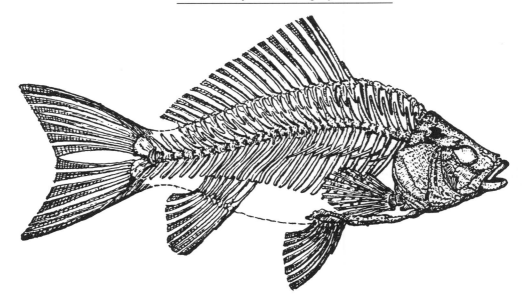

44

The Right Goldfish For You

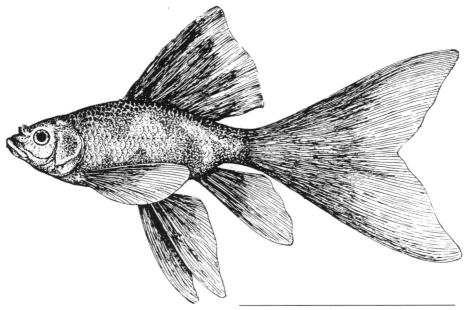

The Japanese Comet Goldfish was probably developed in America.

and even remaining out of water for several hours if kept moist, the common goldfish has a rather long body that is flattened on the sides; a short, wide, and scaleless head; and the usual complement of fins. The fins include the dorsal (on back), the caudal (tail), and anal (small fin nearest tail), all of which are single; and the pectoral fins (nearest head) and ventral fins (near lower center of body), the pectoral and ventral fins being paired.

COMET: An American variety developed from the common goldfish, apparently in the ponds of the Fish Commission in Washington in the early 1880's, the comet has a thin and graceful body capped by a long single tail. A very active fish and the most graceful of all the fancy goldfishes, aquaria housing comets should be covered, especially in the spring.

SHUBUNKIN: Sometimes called the calico fish, the

The Right Goldfish For You

Agard's Wonder Goldfish.

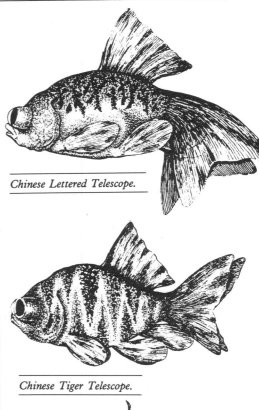

Chinese Lettered Telescope.

Lawson's White Rat.

Head-on view of the Chinese Tiger Telescope.

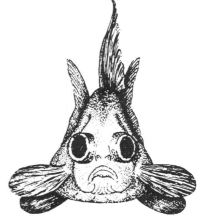

Chinese Tiger Telescope.

The goldfish shown on this page have disappeared from the aquarium scene, but they are the most popular of hundreds of freaks that appeared over the years of the cultivation of goldfish.

The Right Goldfish For You

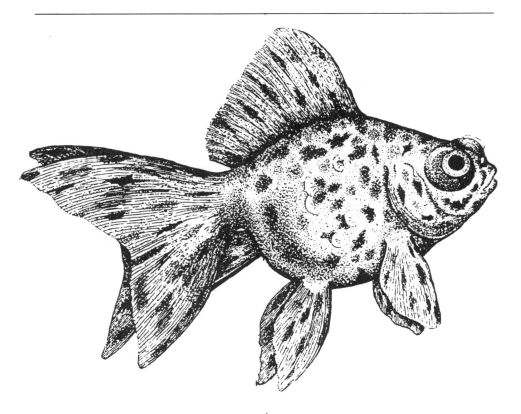

shubunkin combines the colors of red, white, lavender, orange, blue, purple, and black. One of the "scaleless" (transparently scaled) fish referred to previously, shubunkins in good color are one of the most attractive of the goldfish varieties. Unfortunately, the lower priced varieties seldom include shubunkins in good color. Unlike most transparently

This is a magnificent Shubunkin goldfish. It combines the colors of red, white, lavender, orange, blue, purple, and black.

scaled fishes, the shubunkin is very hardy and an active fish. It is not very susceptible to disease and breeds more readily than most fish. It grows to an average length of six inches.

The Right Goldfish For You

FANTAIL: As the name indicates, fantails are fish with double or fan-shaped tails. Fantails are propagated in enormous quantities in the United States, the Orient, and Europe. They have comparatively long bodies and are not burdened with excessively long fins. Kept in a well-maintained aquarium, a

The Japanese Fantail Goldfish, a double- or split-tail variety.

fantail will survive for years. The Japanese type has a deeper body than those produced in this country.

VEILTAIL: In this beautiful variety, symmetry of form is combined with exotic coloring which sets the fish apart from all

The Right Goldfish For You

A show stopper, the Japanese Veiltail. A scaled Japanese Nymph Goldfish.

The Right Goldfish For You

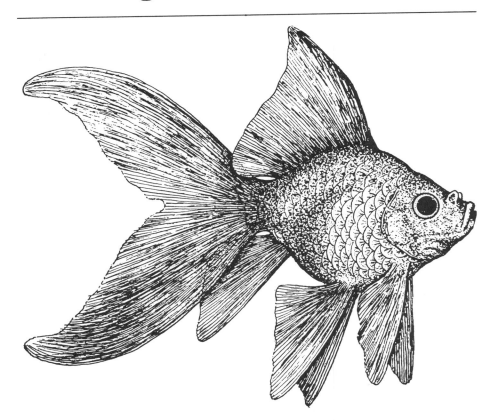

A scaled Japanese Nymph Goldfish.

others. While not so hardy as the fantail and some of the other less exotic varieties, it will endure temperatures around 40 degrees F, provided that they remain constant. It has a tendency to constipation if fed only dried foods and prefers filtered water. Veiltails, also called fringetails, do not attain full beauty until they are fully mature—between two and three years of age. The finnage is silky and flowing, and the tail is divided to the base, each half being at least as long as the body. Colors are blue, violet, red, yellow, and black in the matte variety and red, black, and silver in the scaled variety of this breed.

The Right Goldfish For You

NYMPH: Essentially a single-tail veiltail, the anal fin and tail are single and, instead of drooping, should be carried out straight and well spread. Nymphs are usually found in spawnings of veiltails.

TELESCOPE: A telescope is distinguished by huge, grotesque eyes which protrude from the sides of its head like the headlights of an old car. The eyes vary in shape and in direction, but in most instances they are spherical or conical. Tubular eyes are rare and highly prized. In the early weeks of life the eyes appear normal and it is impossible to predict whether the fish will become telescopes until the eyes begin to develop at any age between two months and two years. A telescope four inches long may have eyes three-fourths of an inch deep. As might be expected, telescopes are handicapped by poor vision, and tanks in which they are housed should have all rough corners

A transparently-scaled Japanese Nymph Goldfish. Essentially, a Nymph is a veiltail without the double or split tail and anal fin. Some of them can be beautiful, but their fins shouldn't droop.

The Right Goldfish For You

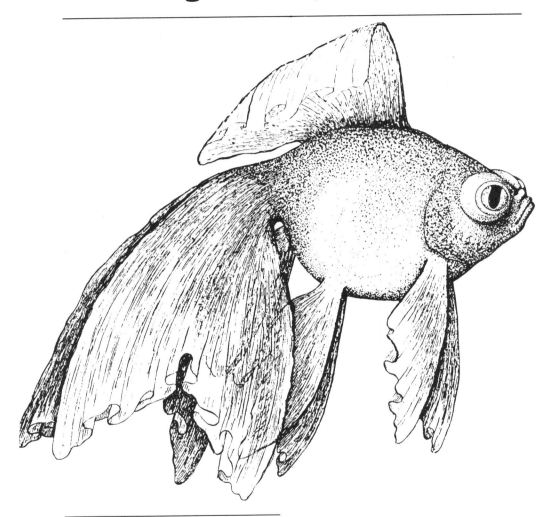

A Chinese Veiltail Telescope Goldfish. This magnificent specimen has wave-like fringes on all its fins.

The Right Goldfish For You

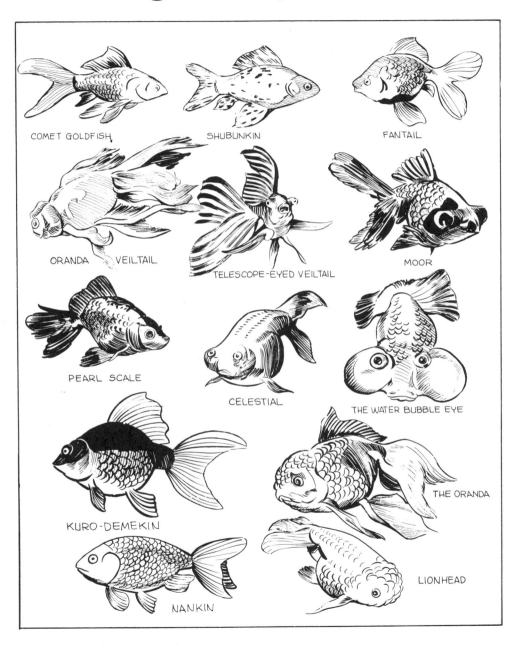

COMET GOLDFISH

SHUBUNKIN

FANTAIL

ORANDA   VEILTAIL

TELESCOPE-EYED VEILTAIL

MOOR

PEARL SCALE

CELESTIAL

THE WATER BUBBLE EYE

KURO-DEMEKIN

THE ORANDA

NANKIN

LIONHEAD

The Right Goldfish For You

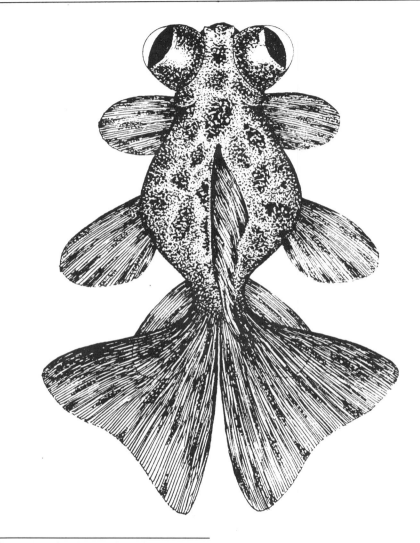

A top view of a Chinese Shubunkin Telescope Goldfish.

The Right Goldfish For You

removed to prevent damage to the eyes. With the exception of the eyes, telescopes resemble veiltails on all other points—medium long head, small mouth and protruding nostrils, a moderately deep body of medium thickness, all fins moderate in length with a tendency to be oval, anal and caudal fins paired, and tail spread out and slightly forked. They are found in both scaled and "scaleless" forms.

CELESTIAL: This is a very incongruous creature—a telescopic fish with its pupils on the top of the eyeballs and lacking a dorsal fin. A very difficult fish to keep and expensive to obtain, the celestial is not recommended for beginners. As in the case of the telescope, the eyes of the young fry appear normal, developing the telescopic appearance at about twelve weeks of age. The pupils gradually turn toward the top of the head later.

MOOR: A telescopic variety, the Moor is readily recognized by its intense velvety black color. In addition to the telescopic eyes, this variety has a large and voluminous double tail.

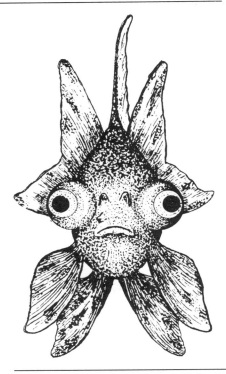

A head-on view of a young Chinese Shubunkin Telescope Goldfish.

LIONHEAD: An example of a great achievement in selective breeding, the lionhead (also called buffalohead) is characterized by a thick raspberry-like growth over the gill plates and head. Lionheads, like the celestials, lack dorsal fins; their bodies are extremely thick and short. The growth on the head seldom begins to appear

The Right Goldfish For You

A Chinese Celestial Telescope Goldfish. Below, a top view of the same fish.

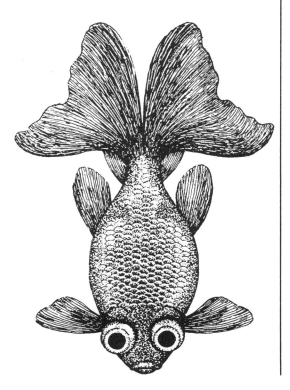

before the fish is six months old and increases in size as long as the fish lives. Lionheads must be kept in well-aerated water as the growth impairs breathing. It is found in the usual red and white colors of the common goldfish, although pearl white bodies and pale yellow heads are not uncommon.

You will find most goldfish in sizes of from two to eight inches long, at prices ranging from under a dollar to over $50 each.

Opposite top: A wakin goldfish. Wakin goldfish are the common goldfish of Japan; they are usually the hardiest and the least expensive of the Japanese varieties. Opposite, bottom left: A calico, or calico fantail, goldfish. Calicos are noted fot their beautiful red and white coloration. Many specimens, like this one, also display blue or black spots. Opposite, bottom right: A shubunkin goldfish. The name shubunkin means "red brocade" or "of many colors with red."

Above and below: Two examples of water bubble eye goldfish. **Opposite:** Peacock goldfish, called kujaku *in Japanese.*

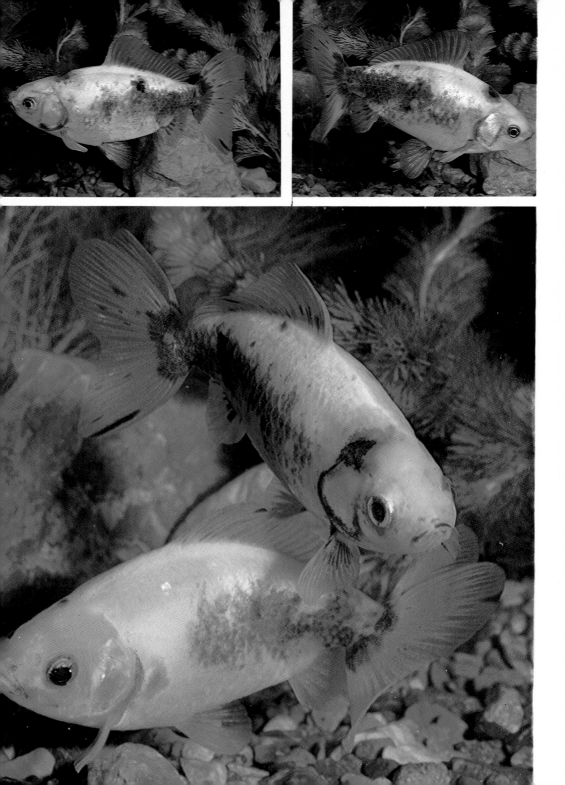

Top series: Various lionhead and oranda head growths. ***Opposite bottom:*** *Note the impressive head growth on this goldfish.* ***Below:*** *Since goldfish are descended from the carp, common goldfish are often mistaken for* koi, *ornamental carp.*

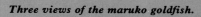

Three views of the maruko goldfish.

An excellent pair of lionhead goldfish. Note the lovely coloration on both of these fish.

A trio of celestial goldfish. The eyes of celestial goldfish turn upward at about 12 weeks of age.

The Right Goldfish For You

Don't look for size; look for quality in color and shape, and always buy the best you can afford.

For a small two-gallon tank you will need only two one-inch fish, a small plant, and just enough sand to cover the bottom. However, in such a small tank it is better to have a little ceramic ornament rather than a plant, as goldfish will invariably pull out almost any plant in their tank that is not firmly rooted or potted. Small fish, however, are not so hard on plants, and it is worth a try with a small plant to see how they act. Otherwise use some sort of small rock or other ornament.

Care and Feeding of Goldfish

Feed your fish only prepared fish food, a small pinch every other day. There is no danger of your fish starving but there is great danger in over-feeding. Watch your fish to see if they eat all of the food, and remove any uneaten particles. Food left too long will decompose and pollute the water.

A Chinese Moor Telescope Goldfish. They are all black.

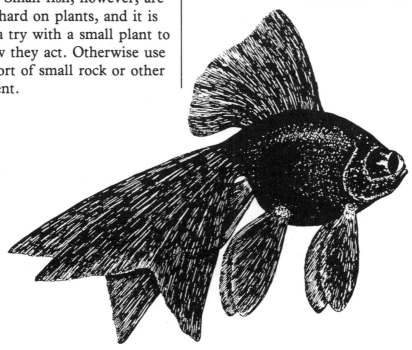

The Right Goldfish For You

An adult Lionhead or Buffalohead Goldfish. Note the missing dorsal fin.

When transferring your fish from one tank to another, care must be taken to see that the water in both tanks is of the same temperature. A sudden change in temperature shocks the fish and weakens it, making the fish susceptible to disease. Never put water directly from the spigot into the fish tank. It is advisable to let the water sit in the room with the tank until it has a chance to become the same temperature as that in the tank. This will also give time for any chlorine that may be in the water to escape.

There is no set rule as to how often to change the water. It is best not to disturb the fish so long as they are comfortable. By

The Right Goldfish For You

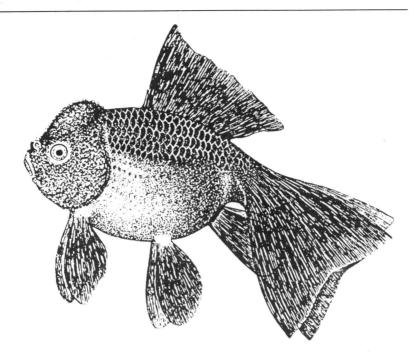

Oranda shishigashira is a Lionhead with a dorsal fin.

watching them, you can soon learn from their actions whether they are comfortable or not. If they come to the top of the water and make a gasping sound as if they were blowing bubbles, and if their gill covers move in quick strokes, they need more oxygen in the water. The simplest way to furnish them this oxygen is to change part of the water. Otherwise, unless it becomes dirty, it is better not to change it. Never use soap or cleansing powder of any kind to wash your tank; use only salt and clear water.

Watch for sick fish and remove them at once. It is best to remove sick fish for several days and treat them individually. It is also wise to treat the rest of the fish, just in case they might have been infected. Wash the tank, ornaments, and plants with salt water, and, if possible, let the tank sun for a day or so before using it again.

Spawning Goldfish

There is no complicated mystery about breeding goldfish. In Nature, the sequence goes something like the following.

In the spring, usually around the middle of April, the male fish begin to frolic through the water playing what looks like a game of tag with the females. A male will single out a female and chase her. The frantic female seems disturbed by this pursuit and seeks a refuge in the fine roots of the plants. There she deposits her eggs. The male follows behind her and hovers over the eggs, depositing the milt (the spermatic fluid of the male fish) which immediately fertilizes the eggs.

A female will lay several hundred eggs at a time, and the breeding season will continue for several months, as long as the males are active. It is possible for one six-inch female to lay as many as 75,000 eggs in a single season. Don't be alarmed. They don't all hatch, and many fry die young.

After the eggs are laid and fertilized, they go through an

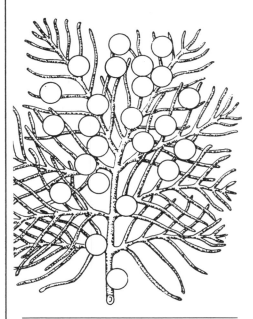

Goldfish spawn attached to the leaf of an aquatic plant. This is a greatly enlarged drawing.

incubation period of from one to two weeks, the length of time depending on the temperature of the water. In an indoor tank at 72 degrees, they hatch in three to four days.

After the eggs hatch, the young fry hide in the roots of the water plants to protect themselves from their parents and other larger fish which would eat them if they had the opportunity. For

Spawning Goldfish

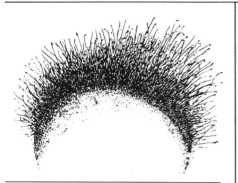

The eggs which are not fertilized are usually attacked by a white hairy fungus, Saprolegnia. *This fungus spreads to healthy eggs unless the water is treated.*

this reason, Nature protects the young fry by camouflaging them with an olive brown color.

The young fish do not eat anything for three days, but they make up for lost time when they do begin. Their appetite is very great, and to ensure rapid growth and brilliant color they should be fed several times a day.

Methods for Breeding Goldfish

The simplest breeding method, and probably the most widely used, is that of merely letting Nature take its course. Stock a pool in the fall or early spring with several fish of nice size and plant plenty of water hyacinths. Spawning will begin as soon as the weather grows warm, and by careful watching you should be able to see the young fry along about the last of April. As soon as the young fry appear, get a shallow pan and scoop up as many as you can catch and put them into a large (15-gallon or more) aquarium. Be sure that the water in the tank is of the same temperature as that in the pool. In fact, it is best to take the water directly from the pool. Several hours of sun each day will help the fish grow and color rapidly, but don't keep them in the sun too long at a time.

Feed the fry several times a day on finely sieved live daphnia, newly hatched brine shrimp, or on fine #000 tropical fish food of high quality. After the fish are two weeks old add wheat flour and chopped earthworms to their diet. After the young fish grow to be an inch or two long, they may be returned to the pool.

However, undoubtedly the best results may be obtained by using the following, more commercial

Spawning Goldfish

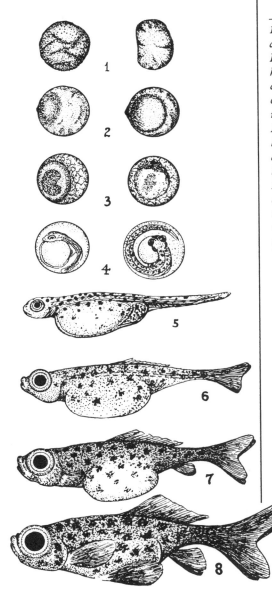

1. Newly exuded egg, not fecundated, wrinkled and unexpanded surface covered with vesicles. Full and lateral views. 2. Egg, four and ten hours after fecundation, showing germination and formation of membrane. 3. Development of embryo and plasmic processes at edge of membrane, 24 and 34 hours after spawning. 4. Development of alevin and yolk-sac, 50 and 58 hours after spawning. 5. Free-swimming alevin attached to the yolk-sac, showing skeleton, partly developed digestive organs and surface colors. Four days old. 6. Alevin five days old; dorsal and caudal fins party developed. 7. Alevin seven days old; pectoral and anal fins developed. 8. The fully developed Telescope fry, ten days old.

method. Place two males and one female in a large tank. In general, the simplest method of determining the sexes is to watch the fish in the breeding season and notice their actions. The males will be chasing the females. The female is much deeper in body. The male has a longer, slimmer body, and when about to spawn he develops white breeding tubercles about the head and gills.

Spawning Goldfish

The aquarium should be clean of vegetation, but nylon spawning mops like those used for killifishes should be added. The female will deposit her eggs in the mop, and the males will fertilize them. As soon as you are sure the spawning is over, place the fish in another tank. If you want more than one hatch, do the same thing over again in a few days with a different aquarium. Let the aquarium with the eggs in it have a few hours of sun every day, and you should soon have a nice collection of young fish.

The Development of Fry

The actual fertilization of the goldfish egg is a very fascinating piece of natural phenomena. By a series of frantic chasings the male pursues the female. The effect of this is to cause the female to release a number of eggs, which, in well-matched pairs, coincides with the release of milt on the part of the male. The eggs are compressed when they are released, but they swell quickly as they absorb the water.

The fertilized egg begins to develop at once, and a fry soon emerges. The rate of development is dependent on the temperature of the water and varies from sixteen days at 65 degrees F to three days at 75 degrees F. The best hatching temperature seems to be 72 degrees F, which means that the babies should appear in about four days. Those eggs which escape fertilization become covered with a fungoid growth and turn white within twelve hours.

The egg can be seen easily with the naked eye and is about the size of a pinhead. The eggs are laid separately and adhere readily to any surrounding objects. Those that fail to attach themselves sink to the bottom. Some breeders remove the plants or mops containing the eggs to another tank, while others prefer to leave the eggs in the water of the spawning tank.

As with most egg-laying fishes in the aquarium, a fry is hatched with an egg sac attached to its chest, so to speak. This egg sac is absorbed slowly during the first forty-eight hours, so during

Diseases and Treatments

this period feeding is unnecessary.

It is not until the third day that the fry can swim, and up until that time it attaches itself vertically to anything within reach.

Once it has reached the free-swimming stage, the fry starts a ceaseless search for food. That is where the aquarist's real problem begins—he must feed hundreds of fish. Most aquarists prefer to feed brine shrimp nauplii. The fry can take the shrimp the moment they become free-swimming, and grow more rapidly on it than any other food. When the fry get to be about an inch long, they can take chopped white worms, then a little later whole white worms. From that time on, a combination of fine dry foods and live foods will keep them growing nicely.

In Nature, fishes are sometimes attacked by diseases and parasitic enemies. Fishes that have been kept under artificial conditions, inbred, and weakened by improper feeding would naturally be more susceptible to the many maladies that are common in the aquatic world. The wonder is that so many of the maladies can, under these conditions, be successfully treated.

The aquarist can by constant watching and observation have the battle half won by catching the disease or trouble in time, diagnosing it properly, and administering the proper treatment at once. Some of the signs that the aquarist should be on the alert for are listless movements, loss of appetite, dorsal fin drooping, caudal or tail fin pinched (when the fish is in the habit of holding its fins well spread), congested or frayed fin (congested fins usually show bloodshot or raw areas), a grayish white slime on the body, bubbles in the excrement, and white spot (ich).

Whenever there is the least doubt in mind, the fish should

Diseases and Treatments

be observed carefully for two or three days and if any condition that may indicate trouble presents itself, the necessary treatment should be given at once and the fish should be moved to private quarters. There is always a possibility that a fish may be suffering from a contagious condition that might spread quickly to the other members of the tank. Then again, the fish may be the carrier of the disease and not be made more than passingly sick while other fish in the aquarium will die from the disease. An ounce of prevention is worth a pound of cure. Move the ailing fish into a sick ward and observe all for any trouble that may break out. Diseases of fish spread rapidly and cause much trouble in short periods of time. Nets used to handle sick fish should be sterilized or, better still, never use with well fish a net that has been put into the sick ward.

The Salt Treatment

Many of the disease-producing organisms of fresh water are unable to live in a moderate salt solution. Others can live a normal life, but during the period of the egg or the larvae or at some free-swimming stage, the mild salt solution will stop their spread.

The kind of salt is of some importance and should be considered. Ordinary table salt on occasion contains chemicals to prevent caking in damp weather. These may be injurious to fish. The best, but not always the easiest to obtain, is real sea-water salt. Even those living on the coast cannot always obtain sea water that is not polluted or diluted to some extent, and this may have as serious a result as the disease itself. The next best is rock salt or evaporated sea salt, but in any event, if it is the salt treatment that is needed, get the infected fish into the salt, whatever type it may be. Some recommend the addition of one-third Epsom salt. This may or may not be beneficial but in any case could do little if any harm. Epsom salt is good for constipation in fish and may be given by dropping a few grains in front of the fish; a small dose

Diseases and Treatments

is all that is necessary. A good solution is one made of one part of natural sea water to five parts of aged tap water or two teaspoons of rock crystal salt to a gallon of water.

Fish will recover more quickly in shallow water and if kept out of bright light. An enamel tray is a very good container. Temperature should be constant. Should the fish not show improvement in four days, increase the strength of the solution gradually for two or three days until it is the equivalent of four teaspoons of salt per gallon or double the strength of the original solution. Let this stand for two days and then begin diluting it to the original strength.

It is often difficult to diagnose and treat diseases of goldfish rapidly enough to save the fish. Your pet shop will have many remedies for common diseases such as ich, and in many cases they will work better than the simple remedies given below. Check with your pet shop if your fish seems to be suffering from a disease and follow the manager's recommendations.

Fin Congestion

Fancy goldfish are probably more liable to attack from this trouble than almost any other disease. They will show an indisposed condition brought on by overfeeding, sudden chill, low temperatures, and long high temperatures. Congested fins are easy to diagnose as the fins become more or less bloodshot—especially where the fins join the body. This is especially true with the tail fin.

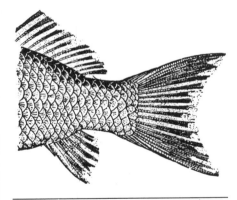

Fins of a goldfish affected with tailrot.

The treatment that has probably given the greatest amount of relief is the salt treatment as already described.

Diseases and Treatments

One-eighth grain of potassium permanganate to a gallon of water has been successful for goldfish. The permanganate should be mixed in glass containers as most other materials may change the chemical structure and cause some form of poisoning in the fish.

Should the red or bloodshot condition be at the base of the tail in the fleshy part, it is a different infection. It will, however, react to the same treatment as above, but treatment must be given quickly.

White Fungus

The fungus spores which cause this disease are generally in all water but do not attack fish until they are in a weakened condition (chilled, protective slime removed by rough swimming at spawning time, handled with dry hands, held in water that has too high a temperature, or bruised in shipment). This disease generally starts at the fins or point of bruise and spreads over the body until it enters the gills, at which point it is fatal. It weakens the fish to a point that they frequently die in the secondary stages of the disease. When white fungus starts spreading on an individual, the fish should be removed at once as the disease is very contagious.

The same treatment may be used for white fungus as for fin congestion. When the fins are frayed and it is necessary to trim them, a sharp knife should be used rather than scissors as the cut will be cleaner. A salt treatment will help prevent a secondary infection.

Raw spots are at times left by the fungus. They may be treated by holding the fish in a wet cloth or towel and painting the spots with two percent solution of tincture of Merthiolate. Let it dry and return the fish to the hospital tank until all signs of infection are gone.

Constipation

Constipation can be the cause of considerable trouble in the aquarium. Constipation is brought on in fish by

Diseases and Treatments

malnutrition or improper feeding. The use of a single food as a constant diet such as oatmeal and foods high in starches may cause constipation.

A bath of half sea salt and half Epsom salt made to the strength of one ounce to the gallon of water will help. The dropping of grains of Epsom salt before the individual until one grain has been taken into the mouth is generally sufficient to relieve the condition. Change the diet to chopped earthworms, spinach, live daphnia, white worms, or a little raw shrimp.

Tail Rot

This disease is first noticeable along the outer edge of the tail fin. Showing up as frayed edges, leaving the ends of the rays exposed, it eats its way into the fleshy part of the tail and is at this stage very serious. If treatment is given soon enough, the fish can be saved and the spread of the disease prevented. As tail rot generally follows after the fish is allowed to get into

a rundown condition, a general building up of the fish's health is necessary and an improvement in the environment is also required.

The same treatment as that for white fungus is, as a rule, good and will generally remedy the condition. Also, the tail of the fish may be dipped into a solution of hydrogen peroxide for a period of two minutes. Put a wet rag around the head and gills of the fish and hold it tightly in the solution; rinse in fresh water and then replace in the aquarium.

Dropsy

The cause of this unsightly as well as troublesome condition is not known with certainty. The fish's abdomen swells and the scales seem to stand away from the body. It does not appear to be contagious, and should one fish be infected the others in the aquarium do not contract the disease. Goldfish are among the species that seem to be more susceptible than others. The victim does not seem to be

Diseases and Treatments

depressed until a day or two before death, although it may be affected for ten days to three weeks before dying. Most fanciers dispose of the infected fish at once as there is no sure cure.

Swim Bladder Trouble

This condition is prevalent among fancy short-bodied goldfish. The victim shows considerable discomfort and rises from the bottom of the aquarium only by violent effort. The fish may lie listlessly at the surface upside down or at any angle at which the body may have stopped. This condition may be brought about by reduced temperatures, whether brought on slowly or rapidly. It may be the result of internal parasites attacking the swim bladder or, in some cases, it may be from fighting.

In any event, when the swim bladder is affected there is not a great deal that can be done. Some relief may be obtained by placing the affected fish in very

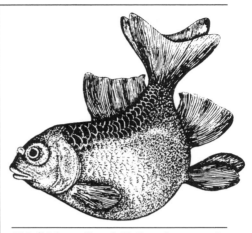

This fish has a distended belly and cannot swim properly. This may be swim bladder trouble or dropsy.

shallow water, just sufficient in which to swim, with one teaspoon of salt to a gallon of water. The fish may be moved into deeper water after a week or two and, if the condition has corrected itself, may be returned to its aquarium. Many fish affected with this trouble have to remain in shallow water permanently. It must be borne in mind that not all cases of lost equilibrium are due to swim bladder trouble. It may be due to an accumulation of gases in the stomach or in the intestines. The treatment for constipation will relieve this condition, and a change of diet should be given.

Diseases and Treatments

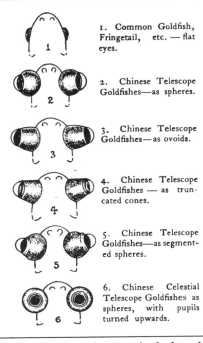

1. Common Goldfish, Fringetail, etc. — flat eyes.

2. Chinese Telescope Goldfishes—as spheres.

3. Chinese Telescope Goldfishes—as ovoids.

4. Chinese Telescope Goldfishes — as truncated cones.

5. Chinese Telescope Goldfishes—as segmented spheres.

6. Chinese Celestial Telescope Goldfishes as spheres, with pupils turned upwards.

These are normal eyes, bred for their configuration. They are not eye inflammations, though they may become inflamed by an injury.

Eye Inflammation

A condition brought on by injuring the eyes in shipping, hitting hard sharp objects in the aquarium, and sometimes fighting.

To prevent permanent loss of sight in some cases, use a cotton swab dipped in a saturated solution of boric acid in water of about 90 degrees. This is applied once daily, and the fish is put into a large aquarium without other fish and without anything against which it may injure its eyes again.

Wounds and Ulcers

Sores appear on fish from time to time. Some are caused by bacterial infections, some by parasites, and some are from fights or chasing during spawning, while others seem to just happen. Those from fights, spawning, etc., can as a rule be cured by the mild salt treatment or a swab dipped in tincture of Merthiolate and gently rubbed over the spots. Other abrasions should be carefully diagnosed. After determining their cause, the proper treatment can be administered.

Ich (*Ichthyophthirius*)

Ich, the bane of many aquarists, is a protozoan parasite

Diseases and Treatments

The head and shoulder of a common goldfish attacked by an infection after the fish lice have left their site. The wounds are ugly and bloody.

spending a part of its life as a cyst, part as a free-swimming larvae, and part as an adult parasite on or imbedded in its host. Of all diseases and parasites common to goldfish, ich is probably the cause of more deaths than any other one thing. Probably more has been written on this parasite than any other, with each author having a "sure cure" or remedy. Ich responds best to a mild treatment of long duration rather than a severe, short treatment.

One ounce of salt (or three level teaspoons) to the gallon, plus raising the temperature to about 80 degrees, will usually cure ich in from five to seven days. Another treatment of merit is to put the fish in a bare tank that is well aerated, hold the temperature to around 80, and add five drops of a five percent solution of methylene blue to the gallon. Two to four drops of a five percent solution of Mercurochrome per gallon at the same temperature is also a well-proven treatment. Any pet shop will have several effective ich cures.

Argulus or Fish Lice

Argulus or fish lice are common parasites on goldfish. The fish louse is a flat, rounded, translucent, scale-like crustacean that is extremely hard to see. They are from one-eighth to one-quarter of an inch in size and very flat through the body. The mouth region is armed with a proboscis which can be inserted into the fish to suck fluids. Argulus differs from copepods in that the female does not carry its

Diseases and Treatments

eggs until they hatch, but lays them on stones or sticks. The eggs are oval, laid end to end in long straight lines, and are covered with a smooth, continuous layer of jelly.

Argulus may be destroyed by the addition of potassium permanganate to the aquarium. The proper ratio is one-fifth grain (by weight) of permanganate per gallon of water.

Index